Stage&screen

D1148748

2 6 NOV 2010

Exclusive Distributors
Music Sales Limited
8/9 Frith Street,
London W1V 5TZ, England.
Music Sales Pty Limited
120 Rothschild Avenue,
Rosebery, NSW 2018,
Australia.

Order No. AM92249
ISBN 0-7119-4374-5
This book © Copyright 1995 by Wise Publications

Book design by Pearce Marchbank, Studio Twenty
Cover illustration by Mark Thomas
Photography by Peter Evans

Your Guarantee of Quality
As publishers, we strive to produce every book to the
highest commercial standards.
This book has been carefully designed to minimise awkward
page turns and to make playing from it a real pleasure.
Particular care has been given to specifying acid-free,
neutral-sized paper made from pulp which have not been
elemental chlorine bleached.
This pulp is from farmed sustainable forests and was
produced with special regard for the environment.
Throughout, the printing and binding have been planned to
ensure a sturdy, attractive publication which should
give years of enjoyment.
If your copy fails to meet our high standards,
please inform us and we will gladly replace it.

Music Sales' complete catalogue describes thousands of
titles and is available in full colour sections by subject, direct
from Music Sales Limited. Please state your areas of interest
and send a cheque/postal order for £1.50 for postage to:
Music Sales Limited, Newmarket Road,
Bury St. Edmunds, Suffolk IP33 3YB.

I Could Have Danced All Night

Words by Alan Jay Lerner
Music by Frederick Loewe

REFRAIN (*very brightly*)

I'll nev-er know _____ what made it so _____ ex-cit ing, _____ Why all at once _____ my heart took flight. _____ I on-ly know _____

C6 Cmaj7 E F♯m7 B7 E Emaj7 E6 E G Am Cdim G9 F Cmaj7 Dm7 C

On The Street Where You Live

Words by Alan Jay Lerner
Music by Frederick Loewe

That could on-ly be **your** room! _____ This

street is like a gar-den and your door a gar-den gate,_____ What a

love-ly place to wait.

REFRAIN (*slowly*)

I have of-ten walked _____ down this street be-fore _____

Fiddler On The Roof

Music by Jerry Bock
Lyrics by Sheldon Harnick

If I Were A Rich Man

Words by Sheldon Harnick
Music by Jerry Bock

Freely

Boi, boi, boi, boi, boi, boi, boi, boi, boi.___

Deliberately (in tempo)

Fm7   Bb7

And it won't make one bit of dif - f'rence

Ebmaj7   Bbm6 C7 Fm   F#dim

If I an - swer right or wrong? When you're rich, they think you real - ly

G7   C7   Reflective, lyrical, soft
F   G7

know.   If I were rich, I'd have the time that I lack, To

rall.   _p_

C   A7   Dm7   G7

sit in the syn - a - gogue and pray; And may be have a seat by the east - ern

wall.

And I'd dis - cuss the ho - ly books with the learn - ed men sev - en ho - urs ev -'ry day; This would be the sweet - est thing of all. _____ (Sigh) IF I WERE A RICH MAN, Dai - dle, dee - dle, dai - dle, dig - guh, dig - guh, dee - dle, dai - dle, dum. All day long I'd bid - dy, bid - dy bum,

Tempo I°

Matchmaker

Words by Sheldon Harnick
Music by Jerry Bock

girl can get burned. So bring me no ring,
Groom me no
(Male:) So bring her a ring,
Groom her a

groom,
Find me no find,
Catch me no catch;
groom,
Find her a find,
Catch her a catch;

Un - less he's a match - less match!
And make her a match - less match!

Sunrise Sunset

Words by Sheldon Harnick
Music by Jerry Bock

Moderately Slow Waltz tempo *(soulful and wistful)*

Thank Heaven For Little Girls

Words by Alan Jay Lerner
Music by Frederick Loewe

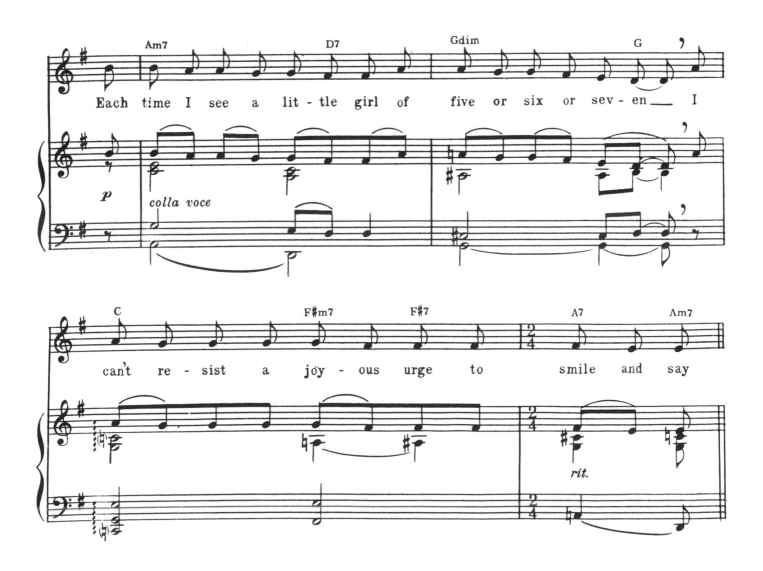

Refrain

I Remember It Well

Words by Alan Jay Lerner
Music by Frederick Loewe

might by some chance be think-ing of it too?_____ That car-riage

ride. You walked me home. You lost a glove. I lost a comb. Ah yes! I re-

mem-ber it well. That bril-liant sky. We had some rain. Those Rus-sian

songs. From sun-ny Spain. Ah yes! I re-mem-ber it well.

Gonna Build A Mountain

Words & Music by Leslie Bricusse & Anthony Newley

Gon-na build a moun-tain Gon-na build it high.
Gon-na build a day-dream (Yeah, Yeah,) Gon-na see it through. (Yeah, Yeah,)
If I build my moun-tain with a lot of care

Bb7   Fm7   Eb   Eb7   Abmaj9

I don't know how I'm gon-na do it on-ly know I'm gon-na
Gon-na build a moun-tain and a day-dream gon-na make 'em both come
And take my day-dream up the moun-tain Hea-ven will be wait-ing

Db9   E7   Cm7   Fm7   Bb7

1 & 2   3
                    ad lib.
try. (Yeah, Yeah,) 2. Gon-na build a there. (Yeah, Yeah,) 4. When I've built that
true. (Yeah, Yeah,) 3. Gon-na build a

colla voce

sfz

Eb   Fm7   Eb   Eb   B7

Hea-ven as I will some day   And the Lord sends Ga - briel

f

E   F#m7   E   F#m7   E   F#m7   E   F#m7

EXTRA VERSES

5.

Gonna build a Heaven from a little hell
Gonna build a Heaven and I know well
With a fine young son who will take my place
There'll be a sun in my Heaven on earth
With the good Lord's grace.

6.

Gonna build a mountain from a little hill.
Gonna build a mountain __ least I hope I will.
Gonna build a mountain __ gonna build it high.
I don't know how I'm gonna do it
I only know I'm gonna try.

Once In A Lifetime

Words & Music by Leslie Bricusse & Anthony Newley

Maestoso

Just once in a life-time__ A

man knows a mo-ment__ One won-der-ful mo-ment When fate takes his hand__

And this is my mo-ment__ My once in a life-time__ When

I can ex-plore a new and ex-cit-ing land.__ For

What Kind Of Fool Am I

Words & Music by Leslie Bricusse & Anthony Newley

Who Can I Turn To?

Words & Music by Leslie Bricusse & Anthony Newley

And may-be to-mor-row _____ I'll find what I'm af-ter_____ I'll

throw off my sor-row beg steal or bor-row my share of laugh-ter._____ With you I could learn to,

with you on a new day,_____ But who can I turn to if you turn a-

way?_____ way?_____

A Wonderful Day Like Today

Words & Music by Leslie Bricusse & Anthony Newley

An Affair To Remember

Words by Harold Adamson & Leo McCarey
Music by Harry Warren

Moderately (with movement)

Because You're Mine

Words by Sammy Cahn
Music by Nicholas Brodszky

kiss that you a - lone may give me. And when we

kiss _____ that is - n't thun - der dear, It's on - ly my poor

heart you hear, and it's ap - plause, BE - CAUSE YOU'RE

MINE! _____ BE-CAUSE YOU'RE MINE! _____

A Certain Smile

Words by Paul Francis Webster
Music by Sammy Fain

Everybody's Talkin'

Words & Music by Fred Neil

shad-ows ___ of their eyes ___ I'm ___ go-in' where the sun ___ keeps shin-in'

thru the pour - in' ___ rain Go - in' where the weath-er ___ suits my

clothes ___ Bank-in' off of the north-east ___ wind Sail-in' on a sum-mer ___

D.S. al Coda

breeze Skip-pin' o-ver the o - cean ___ like a stone. ___

D.S. al Coda

Repeat and fade

♦ *Coda*

— And I won't ___ let you leave my love ___ be - hind ___ No,
I won't ___ let you leave my love ___ be - hind ___ And,
I won't ___ let you leave my love be - hind ___

High Noon

Words by Ned Washington
Music by Dimitri Tiomkin

Love Is A Many Splendoured Thing

Words by Paul Francis Webster
Music by Sammy Fain

The Shadow Of Your Smile

Words by Paul Francis Webster
Music by Johnny Mandel

Three Coins In The Fountain

Words by Sammy Cahn
Music by Jule Styne

Stardust

Words by Mitchell Parish
Music by Hoagy Carmichael

And now the pur-ple dusk of twi-light time Steals a-cross the mea-dows of my heart, High up in the sky the lit-tle stars climb, Al-ways re-mind-ing me that we're a-part. You wandered down the lane and far a-way, Leav-ing me a song that will not

die,　Love is now the star dust of yes-ter-day,　The mus-ic of the years gone by. _____

A7　Dm　C　dim G7

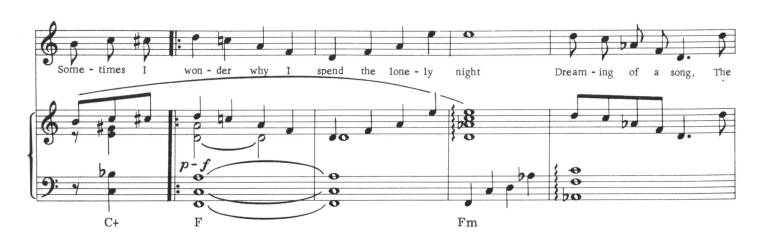

Some-times I won-der why I spend the lone-ly night　Dream-ing of a song, The

C+　F　Fm

mel-o-dy haunts my re-ve-rie,　And I am once a-gain with you _____ When our love was new,

C　Em　F　F6　Fm6　G7 dim G7

and each kiss an in-spir-a-tion, _____　But that was long a-go: now my con-so-la-tion is

G+　C　D7

Lawrence Of Arabia

By Maurice Jarre

Diamonds Are A Girl's Best Friend

Words by Leo Robin
Music by Jule Styne

CHORUS

gives ex-pen-sive jew-els; ___
stones still keep their flick-er; ___

A kiss on the hand may be quite Con-ti-nen-tal, But
There may come a time when a lass needs a law-yer, But

Dia-monds Are A Girl's Best Friend, ___ A kiss may be
Dia-monds Are A Girl's Best Friend, ___ There may come a

grand But it won't pay the rent-al on your hum-ble flat ___ Or
time When a hard boiled em-ploy-er thinks you're aw-ful nice, ___ But

help you at the Au - to - mat. Men grow cold as girls grow
get that "ice" or else no dice. He's your cold guy when stocks grow

old And we all lose our charms in the end. _____ But
high, But be - ware when they start to de - scend. _____ It's

square cut or pear shape, These rocks don't lose their shape, Dia - monds Are A
then that those lous - es Go back to their spous - es, Dia - monds Are A

Girl's Best Friend. _____
Girl's Best Friend.

I Will Wait For You

Words by Normal Gimbel
Music by Michel Legrand

Eternally

Words by Geoffrey Parsons & John Turner
Music by Charles Chaplin

CHORUS

The Bare Necessities

Words & Music by Terry Gilkyson

re - ci - pes_____ that bring the bare ne - ces - si - ties_____ of life._____
rest at ease_____ with just the bare ne - ces - si - ties_____ of life._____

_____ Wher - ev - er I wan - der,_____ Wher - ev - er I roam,
_____ When you pick a paw - paw or pric - kl - y pear,
(3.) So just try to re - lax *(Oh Yeah!)* in my back yard,

I could - n't be fond - er _____ of my big home.
And you prick a raw paw _____ next time be - ware.
If you act like that bee acts _____ you're work - in' too hard.

The bees are buzz - in' in the tree to make some hon - ey just for
Don't pick the prick - ly pear by paw, when you pick a pear, try to use the
Don't spend your time just look - in' a - round for some-thing you want that can't be

me.
claw.
found.

You look un-der the rocks and plants and take a glance at the
But you don't need to use the claw when you pick a pear of the
When you find out you can live with-out it and go a-long not

fan-cy ants,___ Then may-be try a few.
big paw-paw,___ Have I giv-en you a clue?
think-in' a-bout___ it. I'll tell you some-thing true.

The bare ne-

ces-si-ties of life will come to you,_____ they'll come to

1.2.

you!___ 2.3. Look for the

(tacet)

3.

you!___

I Wan'na Be Like You

Words & Music by Richard M. Sherman & Robert B. Sherman

Chim Chim Cher-ee

Words & Music by Richard M. Sherman & Robert B. Sherman

CHORUS

Chim chim-in-ey, chim chim-in-ey, chim chim cher-ee! A sweep is as luck-y, as luck-y can be. Chim chim-in-ey, chim chim-in-ey, chim chim cher-oo! Good luck will rub off when I shakes 'ands with

you,   Or   blow   me   a   kiss   and   that's   luck - y,   too.

VERSE

Now,   as   the   lad - der   of
I   choose   me   bris - tles   with

life   'as   been   strung,   You   may   think   a   sweep's   on   the   bot - tom-most
pride,   yes,   I   do: A   broom   for   the   shaft   and   a   brush   for   the

rung. Though   I   spends   me   time   in   the   ash - es   and   smoke,   In
flue. Though   I'm   cov - ered   with   soot   from   me   'ead   to   me   toes,   A

this 'ole wide world there's no 'ap - pi - er bloke.
sweep knows 'e's wel - come wher - ev - er 'e goes.

Up where the smoke is all bill - ered and curled, 'Tween pave - ment and

stars, is the chim - ney sweep world. When there's 'ard - ly no day nor

'ard - ly no night, There's things 'alf in shad - ow and 'alf - way in

them wot sings, "Chim chim cher - ee, chim cher - oo!"

Chim chim - in - ey, chim chim, cher - ee, chim cher - oo!

PROLOGUE VERSION

Room 'ere for everyone, gather around;
The constable's responstable! Now, 'ow does that sound?
Ullo, Miss Lark, I've got one for you:
Miss Lark loves to "wark" in the park with Andrew!
Ah, Missus Corey, a story for you:
Your daughters were shorter than you, but they grew!
Dear Miss Persimmon, – (pause) – winds in the east – there's a mist coming in,
Like something is brewing and 'bout to begin.
Can't put my finger on what lies in store,
But I feel what's to 'appen all 'appened before.

THE "SIDEWALK ARTIST" VERSION

Chim chiminey, chim chiminey, chim chim cheroo!
I does what I likes and I likes what I do.
Today I'm a screever and as you can see,
A screever's an artist of 'ighest degree.
And it's all me own work from me own memory.
Chim chiminey, chim chiminey, chim chim cheroo!
I drawers what I likes and I likes what I drew.
No remuneration do I ask of you,
But me cap would be glad of a copper or two,
Me cap would be glad of a copper or two.

96

A Spoonful Of Sugar

Words & Music by Richard M. Sherman & Robert B. Sherman

snap! The job's a game; _____ And ev-'ry task you un-der-
bits of twine and twig. _____ Though quite in-tent in his pur-
buzz-ing to and fro _____ Be-cause they take a lit-tle

take Be-comes a piece of cake, A
suit, He has a mer-ry tune to toot; He
nip From ev-'ry flow-er that they sip, And

lark! A spree! It's ver-y clear to see
knows a song Will move the job a-long,
hence, they find Their task is not a grind,

CHORUS

That a
For a spoon-ful of su-gar helps the med-i-cine go
For a

98

The Ugly Bug Ball

Words & Music by Richard M.Sherman & Robert B.Sherman

Steady 4

Once a lone-ly cat-er-pil-lar sat and cried, to a sym-pa-thet-ic bee-tle by his side, 'I've got no-bod-y to hug— I'm such an ug-ul-ly bug!' Then a spi-der and a dra-gon fly re-plied 'If you're

Hey There

Words & Music by Richard Adler & Jerry Ross

Goldfinger

Words by Leslie Bricusse & Anthony Newley
Music by John Barry

Live And Let Die

Words & Music by McCartney

Slowly

When you were young, and your heart was an op-en book

You used to say live and let live (You know you did, you know you did, you know you

did___) But in this ev-er chang-ing world___ in which we live___ in makes you

give in and cry___ Say live and let die___

G   Bm   C   D7   D7(9b)

G   Bm   C   D11   D7(9b)

G   Bm   C   A7

D7   Am   D7   Bb/D

live and let die___ live and let die___ live and let

G   C/G   Gdim   G7   G   C/G

To Coda ⊕ *(double tempo)*

die___

Gdim   Gm

(f)

What does it mat - ter to ya

mf

C7

when you got a job to do,___ you got - ta do it well___

G7   D7

107

You got - ta give the oth - er fel - low hell.

Singin' In The Rain

Words by Arthur Freed
Music by Nacio Herb Brown

sun's in my heart And I'm rea - dy for love. Let the storm - y clouds

chase Ev-'ry-one from the place, Come on with the rain, I've a

smile on my face. I'll walk down the lane With a hap - py re-frain, And

sing-in', just sing-in' in the rain. rain.

1 & 2 *to Interlude* **3** *Last time*

INTERLUDE

1 Why am I smil-in' and why do I sing? Why does De-cem-ber seem
2 Why do they call me the boy with the smile? When did I find out that

sun-ny as spring? Why do I get up each morn-ing to start
Life is worth while? Why do I treat all my trou-bles with scorn?

Hap-py and het up, with joy in my heart? Why is each new task a
See-ing the rain-bow be-fore it is born. Why am I sure all my

tri-fle to do? Be-cause I am liv-ing a life full of you.
dreams will come true? Be-cause I am bank-ing my whole world on you.

Days Of Wine And Roses

Words by Johnny Mercer
Music by Henry Mancini

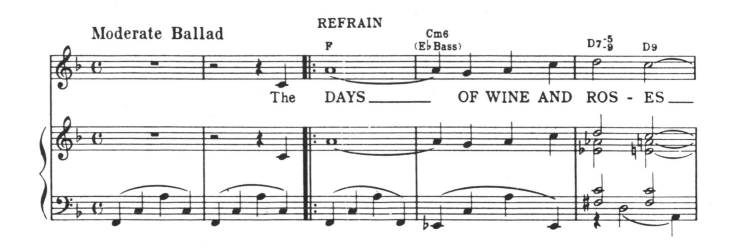

Love Is A Song

Words by Larry Morey
Music by Frank Churchill

fleet - ing, Hope may die, yet love's beau - ti - ful mu - sic, Comes each

day like the dawn. _____ Love is a song that nev - er ends;

One sim-ple theme re - peat - ing, Like the voice of a heav-en-ly

choir_ love's sweet mu-sic flows on. _____ on. _____

Smile

Words by John Turner & Geoffrey Parsons
Music by Charles Chaplin

Smile tho' your heart is ach - ing, Smile ev - en tho' it's break - ing,

When there are clouds in the sky you'll get by, If you smile thro' your

fear and sor - row, Smile and may - be to - mor - row you'll see the sun come shin - ing

Let It Be

Words & Music by John Lennon & Paul McCartney

What Are You Doing The Rest Of Your Life?

Words by Alan & Marilyn Bergman
Music by Michel Legrand

123

Never On Sunday

Words by Dilly Towns
Music by Manos Hadjidakis

The Song From Moulin Rouge
(Where Is Your Heart)

Words by William Engvick
Music by Georges Auric

Somewhere My Love (Lara's Theme)

Words by Paul Francis Webster
Music by Maurice Jarre

Over The Rainbow

Words by E.Y. Harburg
Music by Harold Arlen

Evergreen

Words by Paul Williams
Music by Barbra Streisand

mean-ing of _____ one love, _____ age-less and ev - er _____ ev - er - green. _____

Bright Eyes

Words & Music by Mike Batt

Fairly slowly with expression

death down-stream   oh is it a dream?
hills un - seen   or is it a dream?

There's a fog a - long___ the hor - i - zon
There's a high___ wind___ in the trees___

a strange glow in ___ the sky ___   and
a cold sound in ___ the air ___   and

no - bo - dy seems ___ to know where you go   and what does it
no - bo - dy ev - er knows when you go   and where do you

Take That Look Off Your Face

Music by Andrew Lloyd Webber
Lyrics by Don Black

When I Grow Too Old To Dream

Words by Oscar Hammerstein II
Music by Sigmund Romberg

More Than You Know

Words & Music by William Rose & Edward Eliscu
Music by Vincent Youmans

Tell Me On A Sunday

Music by Andrew Lloyd Webber
Lyrics by Don Black

Printed in Malta by Progress Press Co. Ltd 12/06 (60658)